DAILY
MEDITATION
&
PERSONAL
JOURNAL

"My Soul Follows Hard After Thee"

TOMMY TENNEY

DAILY
MEDITATION
&
PERSONAL
JOURNAL

"My Soul Follows Hard After Thee"

Includes excerpts from:

St. Augustine · Bernard of Clairvaux · Jacob Boeme

Francis de Sales · Henry Drummond · Jonathan Edwards

François Fénelon · Jeanne Guyon · St. John of the Cross

Julian of Norwich · C.S. Lewis · Leonard Ravenhill

A.W. Tozer · Sadhu Sundar Singh

Destiny Image₍ₐ₎ Publishers, Inc.
P.O. Box 310
Shippensburg, PA 17257-0310

"Speaking to the Purposes of God for This Generation
and for the Generations to Come"

ISBN 0-7684-2040-7

For Worldwide Distribution
Printed in the U.S.A.

5 6 7 8 9 / 10 09 08 07 06 05

This book and all other Destiny Image, Revival Press, Mercy Place, Fresh Bread, and Treasure House books are available at Christian bookstores and distributors worldwide.

For a U.S. bookstore nearest you, call **1-800-722-6774**.
For more information on foreign distributors, call **717-532-3040**.
Or reach us on the Internet: **http://www.reapernet.com**

Thoughts From a Fellow God Chaser

Pages from the journals of explorers allow readers to vicariously travel with them to unfrequented locales. Those same pages become a road map to some who actually retrace the steps of the pioneering adventurer. They are not content to just mentally visit distant locations; they want to experience them firsthand.

Reading pages written by "pioneers of His presence" has fueled the fire of my own passion for the pursuit of His presence since I was a young lad. I will never forget the first time I read Leonard Ravenhill's book, *Why Revival Tarries*. I still remember what the cover looked like, and I can still quote entire pages that were burned into my 16-year-old mind. I remember desiring to know God like Ravenhill and Tozer did.

As I grew older I discovered other "pioneers," and I was amazed to find a long lineage of them stretching all the way back to the apostle Paul. Perhaps he was the first New Testament model we were given. By his pursuit in the spirit of what he missed in the flesh he showed us the way and told us to "follow him as he follows Christ" (see 1 Cor. 11:1). Paul did not fraternize with the earthly body of Jesus as did the disciples. Neither have the generations of God chasers since him had that opportunity. But nothing deterred their passionate pursuit of His presence. Paul's words have become the mantra for those mourning for the manifest presence of their Lord. "Oh, that I might know Him" (see Phil. 3:10).

Predating Paul was Moses and his quest for the "glory." How often I've wanted to join him in the secret cleft of the rock while God passed close by.

"Show me Your glory" has been the borrowed prayer of God chasers for centuries. Their tales of pursuit were often written into their own journals. Some of the Holy Writ was birthed in this manner. There are some new names I have included here to familiarize you more with their "paths to His presence." I have discovered some new paths myself. There is brand-new insight that I have never published before. What you'll find is that there are many paths to Him, whether it be the contemplative and quiet or the confrontive and bold.

Many people are content to let others push the envelope of spiritual experience. They will perhaps later read the reports of these spiritual explorers and make a mental visit through their eyes and ears. If that describes you, then this book will have only some value. But if you are hungry for His presence to become real to you, then you will use this book and the writings of these "God chasers" as your personal road map to the Holy of Holies. We have left space for you to leave landmarks for yourself or others to come back and retrace the path you took.

There are untapped regions in the "heights and depths" of Christ. Just when you think you know Him, you'll discover a heretofore hidden aspect of His exceeding majesty. So I encourage you to "run" and "write." Run to Him, and write about Him.

Running and Writing,
Tommy Tenney

Helpful Tips for Your Chase

The purpose of this journal is to introduce you to a new way of spiritual enrichment. It will not be enough to simply read the individual quotes, write a few words, and then move on to the next page. The author and the publishers want to encourage you to prayerfully meditate on these powerful truths. As you do so, this journal will become a resource that will help move you to new levels of intimacy with the Lord Jesus and enable you to return to those new levels.

To Learn His Presence

It is our hope that this journal will help you live in the presence of the Lord every day. It is not intended to simply add new truth to a bag that is already full; rather, it is our desire that it will bring you to a place of new experiences with God.

But it will require that you spend time thinking on the insights of each individual quote, feeling them in your heart, contemplating on their spiritual meaning, applying them to your life, and ultimately letting them lead you to a quiet place of prayer and communion with your Divine Lover, the Lord Jesus.

Begin Your Journey

Few of us have the opportunity for quiet meditation and personal contemplation every day. Therefore, the pages are not dated. It is important that you use this journal when you have the time to give yourself to prayer and meditation. It will not help you if you simply make this experience a part of a daily regimen of religious duty.

When you have the time to allow the Holy Spirit to move in your heart and speak to you, you will find its greatest impact on your life.

To begin the journey, it is imperative that you find a quiet place where you can get alone with your journal, your Bible, and your Lord. Read each quote several times, making sure that you have captured the essence of the writer's thoughts. Do not be content with a casual glance before quickly moving on to the next quote. Allow the Spirit of the Lord to enter your thought processes and bring fresh insight. Let the words become a prayer that is formed on your lips.

The practice of contemplative prayer is certainly a lost art in our Western society. We are used to having our spiritual food gathered, prepared, cooked, and delivered to our table by our favorite preachers of the day. This journal will provide you with an opportunity to break out of this rut.

You might want to talk to your friends about the quote and get their thoughts and reactions. How about memorizing the quote so that you can think on it during the day?

Come back to these words several times. Do not be satisfied with only one look. Often, days down the road, fresh meaning and application will come to you.

Here are a few questions that will help guide you in your search:

1. What is the main focus and intent of the author's words?
2. How does this concept apply to my life?
3. What Scripture verses will lead me into further application of this truth?
4. What circumstances have I gone through that enrich the meaning of these statements?
5. Are there any particular areas of my life that need adjustment so that I can move into a new level of experiencing the power of this truth?
6. What is preventing me right now from experiencing the reality of these powerful insights?
7. How can I form the truths of this quote into a personal prayer to the Lord?

Perhaps a good landmark to begin with would be these words, which Francis de Sales wrote in his *Introduction to the Devout Life*:

"A blind man when in the presence of his prince will preserve a reverential demeanour if told that the king is there, although unable to see him; but practically, what men do not see they easily forget, and so readily lapse into carelessness and irreverence. Just so, my child, we do not see our God, and although faith warns us that He is present, not beholding Him with our mortal eyes, we are too apt to forget Him, and act as though He were afar: for, while knowing perfectly that He is everywhere, if we do not think about it, it is much as though we knew it not. And therefore, before beginning to pray, it is needful always to rouse the soul to a steadfast remembrance and thought of the Presence of God. This is what David meant when he exclaimed, 'If I climb up to Heaven, Thou art there, and if I go down to hell, Thou art there also!" [Ps. 139:8] And in like manner Jacob, who, beholding the ladder which went up to Heaven, cried out, 'Surely the Lord is in this place and I knew it not' [Gen. 28:16] meaning thereby that he had not thought of it; for assuredly he could not fail to know that God was everywhere and in all things. Therefore, when you make ready to pray, you must say with your whole heart, 'God is indeed here' " (70).

*R*epentance prepares us for His presence. In fact, you cannot live in His presence without repentance.

Good things have become the enemy of the best things. I challenge you and release you right now as you read these words to let your heart be broken by the Holy Ghost. It's time for you to make your life holy. Quit watching what you used to watch; quit reading what you used to read if you are reading it more than you read His Word. He must be your first and greatest hunger.

(*The God Chasers*, 14)

Day

Date

Time

Location

*T*here is much more of God available than we have ever known or imagined, but we have become so satisfied with where we are and what we have that we don't *press in* for God's best. Yes, God is moving among us and working in our lives, but we have been content to comb the carpet for crumbs as opposed to having the abundant loaves of hot bread God has prepared for us in the ovens of Heaven! He has prepared a great table of His presence in this day, and He is calling to the Church, "Come and dine."

(The God Chasers, 22)

_____
Day

_____
Date

_____
Time

_____
Location

God is everywhere, but *He doesn't turn His face and His favor everywhere.* That is why He tells us to seek His face. Yes, He is present with you every time you meet with other believers in a worship service, but how long has it been since your hunger caused you to crawl up in His lap, and like a child, to reach up and take the face of God to turn it toward you? Intimacy with Him! That is what God desires, and His face should be our highest focus.

(*The God Chasers*, 38)

Day

Date

Time

Location

We all should be willing to work for the Lord, but it is a matter of grace on God's part. I am of the opinion that we should not be concerned about working for God until we have learned the meaning and the delight of worshiping Him. A worshiper can work with eternal quality in his work. But a worker who does not worship is only piling up wood, hay and stubble for the time when God sets the world on fire.

(A.W. Tozer, *Worship and Entertainment*, 16)

_____
Day

_____
Date

_____
Time

_____
Location

_____

_____

_____

_____

_____

_____

_____

_____

_____

_____

_____

A iden Wilson Tozer was born April 21, 1897, on a small farm among the spiny ridges of western Pennsylvania. Within a few short years, Tozer, as he preferred to be called, would earn the reputation and title of a "20th-century prophet."

When he was 15 years old, Tozer's family moved to Akron, Ohio. One afternoon as he walked home from his job at Goodyear, he overheard a street preacher say, "If you don't know how to be saved...just call on God." When he got home, he climbed the narrow stairs to the attic where, heeding the preacher's advice, Tozer was launched into a lifelong pursuit of God.

Tozer's forte was his prayer life, which often found him walking the aisles of a sanctuary or lying facedown on the floor. He noted, "As a man prays, so is he." To him the worship of God was paramount in his life and ministry. "His preaching as well as his writings

_____

_____

_____

_____

_____

_____

_____

_____

_____

_____

_____

_____

_____

_____

_____

_____

_____

_____

_____

were but extensions of his prayer life," comments Tozer biographer James L. Snyder. An earlier biographer noted, "He spent more time on his knees than at his desk."

In a small cemetery in Akron, Ohio, his tombstone bears this simple epitaph: "A Man of God."

Some wonder why Tozer's writings are as fresh today as when he was alive. It is because, as one friend commented, "He left the superficial, the obvious and the trivial for others to toss around....[His] books reach deep into the heart."

For almost 50 years, Tozer walked with God. Even though he is gone, he continues to speak, ministering to those who are eager to experience God. As someone put it, "This man makes you want to know and feel God."

Tozer's book, _The Pursuit of God_, has always been a favorite of mine.

*I*f we can get hungry, then He can make us holy. Then He can put the pieces of our broken lives back together. But our hunger is the key. So when you find yourself digging for crumbs in the carpet at the House of Bread, you should be praying, "Lord, stir up a firestorm of hunger in me."

(The God Chasers, 32)

Day

Date

Time

Location

R etire from the world each day to some private spot, even if it be only the bedroom (for a while I retreated to the furnace room for want of a better place). Stay in the secret place till the surrounding noises begin to fade out of your heart and a sense of God's presence envelops you. Deliberately tune out the unpleasant sounds and come out of your closet determined not to hear them. Listen for the inward Voice till you learn to recognize it.

(A.W. Tozer, *Worship and Entertainment*, 45)

_____
Day

_____
Date

_____
Time

_____
Location

"If you seek His face, what you get is His favor." The Church has enjoyed the omnipresence of God, but now you can experience moments of visitation by His *manifest presence*. It makes your hair stand up on end. It runs off demonic forces. But it entices God chasers to run toward...Him!

(Tommy Tenney)

	Day
	Date
	Time
	Location

I just want to find out where He's going so I can position myself at the place where He is going to break open. There is an element of sovereignty in God's choice of places. *Nobody on earth strikes the match for burning bushes.* Only God can do that. Our part consists of wandering through the wilderness until we find that spot, and then to remember to take off our shoes because we've stumbled onto holy ground.

(*The God Chasers*, 55)

Day

Date

Time

Location

God is looking for someone who is willing to tie a rope around an ankle and say, "If I perish, I perish; but I am going to see the King. I want to do everything I can to go behind that veil. I'm going to put on the blood, I'm going to repent, I'm going to do everything I can because I'm tired of knowing *about* Him. *I want to know Him. I've got to see His face.*"

(*The God Chasers*, 62)

*A*nd the people stood afar off, and Moses drew near unto the thick darkness where God was (Exodus 20:21).

The people saw the lightning and heard the thunder—and they shrank back in fear. Instead of pursuing His glory, they ran from Him. So the result of their running from holy intimacy was that they died before they entered the promised land. As my friend David Ravenhill would say, "They drank from the river but died in the wilderness." They chose distant respect over intimate relationship.

(Tommy Tenney)

The Lord looked down from heaven upon the children of men, to see if there were any that did understand, and seek God (Psalm 14:2).

Too often we seek a "word" about us from the prophetic tense. How often do we seek a "word" about Him from the "presence" tense? There are those among us who can reveal the secrets of men's hearts. Where are those among us who can reveal the secrets of God's heart? Are there any who understand, who seek after God?

(Tommy Tenney)

Day

Date

Time

Location

*M*y soul followeth hard after Thee: Thy right hand upholdeth me (Psalm 63:8). "Mary had a little lamb, whose fleece was white as snow....And everywhere that Mary went, the lamb was sure to go." That is, until the Lamb said, "I must be about my Father's business." Now Mary must follow the Lamb. "These are they which follow the Lamb" (Rev. 14:4). Our passion must be following Him. I join with the psalmist: "My soul followeth hard after Thee, O God." I confess, I am a *God chaser.*

(Tommy Tenney)

Day

Date

Time

Location

*A*nd he said unto Him, *If Thy presence go not with me, carry us not up hence* (Exodus 33:15).

"If You're not going, I'm not going!" Rings true, doesn't it? "Where you go, I will go." Sound familiar? It's the mantra of men and women on a mission: the pursuit of His presence. "Lord, If You don't go, don't expect me to go. I'm staying with You. I'm only happy in Your presence." Let this God chaser become a God catcher.

(Tommy Tenney)

Day

Date

Time

Location

I know there's more because there are people who encountered the "more" and were changed forever—God chasers! I pray, "Lord, I want to see You like John saw You! I want to know You like Paul knew You!"

(Tommy Tenney)

Day

Date

Time

Location

Satan's most successful trick is to get us to race to false finish lines. He works tirelessly to get us to stop short and say, "We've made it!" He delights when he sees us fall or pull over to the wayside only to notice at the last moment that *the finish line is still ahead.* The apostle knew of what he spoke when he said, "I press toward the mark, forgetting those things that are behind" (see Phil. 3:13-14).

(*The God Chasers*, 73)

*I*f My people, who are called by My name, will humble themselves and pray and seek My face... (2 Chronicles 7:14 NIV).

There is a step beyond prayer. It's the place of seeking His face—not just His hands, not just His blessings and benefits, but seeking Him and His face. For too long we've wanted Him to slip His hand out from under the veil to dispense our allowance, while He has longed for us to enter in to behold Him and worship Him. If you get His face, you gain His favor. His hands bless where His favor flows.

(Tommy Tenney)

Remember, there is no magic in faith or in names. You can name the name of Jesus a thousand times; but if you will not follow the nature of Jesus the name of Jesus will not mean anything to you. We cannot worship God and live after our own nature. It is when God's nature and our nature begin to harmonize that the power of the name of God begins to operate within us.

(A.W. Tozer, *Worship and Entertainment*, 7-8)

Day

Date

Time

Location

C hrist says, "Give me All....I have not come to torment your natural self, but to kill it. No half-measures are any good. I don't want to cut off a branch here and a branch there, I want to have the whole tree down."

And the first job each morning consists simply in shoving [all your wishes and hopes] back; in listening to that other voice, taking that other point of view, letting that other larger, stronger, quieter life come flowing in.

We can only do it for moments at first.

(C.S. Lewis, excerpts from *Mere Christianity*)

Day

Date

Time

Location

_____

_____

_____

_____

_____

_____

_____

_____

_____

_____

_____

_____

_____

C.S. **Lewis** will be remembered as one of the most important Christian thinkers of the twentieth century. He was born in Ireland in 1900, and the major part of his adult years were spent as a Fellow of Magdalen College, Oxford, where he taught medieval literature. It was in 1931 that he was "surprised by joy,"—Lewis' own description of his conversion to Christianity. A brilliant scholar and writer, Lewis used his talents to reach thousands through the printed and spoken word.

He and a group of friends (including J.R.R. Tolkien, author of *Lord of the Rings*) gathered once a week to share their writings. During those years Lewis produced his famous

_____

_____

_____

_____

_____

_____

_____

_____

_____

_____

_____

_____

_____

_____

_____

_____

_____

_____

_____

work *The Screwtape Letters*. In the early 1940's he delivered talks on various Christian topics over British radio. His fame grew throughout Great Britain and spread to the United States. Out of those talks came the book *Mere Christianity*, a penetrating work of Christian apologetics. Countless Christians point to this book as an essential part of their faith journey. If sales are an indication of popularity, then C.S. Lewis—even 30 years after his death—is one of the most popular Christian thinkers of the twentieth century. Quotes from C.S. Lewis have inspired me. They have been "lights" on the path of pursuing God.

The great danger for [beginners in the spiritual life] will be to become satisfied with their religious works and with themselves.

They would prefer to teach rather than to be taught.

Their hearts grow attached to the feelings they get from their devotional life. They focus on the affect, and not on the substance of devotion.

(St. John of the Cross, excerpts from *The Dark Night of the Soul*)

Day

Date

Time

Location

Born in Fantiveros, Castile, Spain, **John** became a Carmelite monk in 1564. He studied philosophy and theology at the Carmelite college in Salamanca, one of Europe's leading universities. In 1567, the year he was ordained, he met with Teresa of Avila. Teresa saw great potential in John and put him in charge of the order. She admired his rigorous lifestyle and leadership ability. She was not disappointed, as John was able to establish several new orders.

It was during this time that he was named "John of the Cross," as a result of his suffering and commitment. He spent the rest of his life in the service of the Catholic Reform through his leadership and many writings. He was eventually arrested and put in confinement by those who opposed the reform. It was in confinement that his most famous work,

_____

_____

_____

_____

_____

_____

_____

_____

_____

_____

_____

_____

_____

_____

_____

_____

_____

_____

_____

_____

The Dark Night of the Soul, was written. It describes the work of God upon the soul—not through joy and light, but through sorrow and darkness. The concept of the "dark night" has become an integral part of understanding the spiritual journey. Though he died four centuries ago, John of the Cross continues to exercise a significant influence on Christian spirituality.

I would say that John of the Cross illuminated the "dark night of the soul" and made it understandable. In times of great sorrow in my life has come great understanding. I would not want to go back through those times…but I would not trade what I learned for anything. Ask Daniel about his lion's den…or the three Hebrews about the furnace. Facing those experiences was a dark night. But, in them, they "caught" Him.

Asoul which is deep in prayer may experience profound temptations and find itself powerless to prevent them....This happens from one of three causes.

Day

Date

Time

Location

The first cause is the physical pleasure the body takes in spiritual things.

The second cause is the devil.

The third cause is an inordinate fear of impure thoughts.

When the soul enters into the dark night, all these things are put under control. The flesh will be quieted, the devil will be silent, and the fear will subside, all because of the fact that God takes away all of the sensory pleasure, and the soul is purified in the absence of it.

When their delight comes to an end, these persons are very anxious and frustrated just as an infant is angry when it is taken away from its mother's breast.

(St. John of the Cross, excerpts from *The Dark Night of the Soul*)

God interposes himself as it were, between me and myself; He separates me from myself; He desires to be nearer to me by his pure love than I am to myself. He would have me look upon this "me" as a stranger; He would have me escape from its walls, sacrifice it whole to Him, returning it absolutely and unconditionally to Him from whom I received it.

(Fénelon, *Spiritual Progress*)

_____
Day

_____
Date

_____
Time

_____
Location

François de Salignac de la Mothe Fénelon was a prominent member of the court of Louis XIV, serving as the tutor of the Duke of Burgundy. A man of high esteem in the Church, Fénelon was appointed archbishop of Cambrai in 1695. During this time he became acquainted with Madame Guyon and was greatly influenced by her and others of the Quietist movement in France. (Quietism stressed the importance of complete detachment from the things of this world.)

Fénelon's defense of Quietism (in his work *Maxims of the Saints*) created a controversy that eventually led to his denunciation by Pope Innocent XII for "having loved God too

_____

_____

_____

_____

_____

_____

_____

_____

_____

_____

_____

_____

_____

_____

_____

_____

_____

_____

_____

much, and man too little." That is quite an indictment! His piety probably convicted those around him. I would like to plead guilty to that offense. He was banished by Louis XIV and received his appointment to a local church where he earned the reputation of being an ideal pastor. It is obvious that he loved people by the fact that he successfully pastored. Religion, politics, and the pursuit of God often don't mix.

Fénelon corresponded with many prominent figures of his day, serving as their spiritual director. His letters were compiled and published for the edification of others. The major theme of his writing is complete love of God.

G od, who wants to strip the soul to perfect it, and will pursue it relentlessly toward a purer love, makes it really pass these tests of itself, and does not let it rest until it has taken away all reversion and all self-support from its love.

(Fénelon, *Christian Perfection*, 149)

Day

Date

Time

Location

It is not with a doubtful consciousness, but one fully certain that I love thee, O Lord. Thou hast smitten my heart with thy Word, and I have loved thee. And see also the heaven, and earth, and all that is in them—on every side they tell me to love thee, and they do not cease to tell this to all men, "so that they are without excuse."

(St. Augustine, *Confessions*, Chapter VI, 8.330)

Day

Date

Time

Location

St. Augustine, the bishop of Hippo, was the great doctor of the Latin Church. He was born in North Africa in 354, the son of a pagan father and a devoutly religious mother. He was brought up as a Christian and at the age of 16 went to Carthage to complete his education in law. In 375 he became interested in philosophy and abandoned his Christian heritage. A skilled orator, Augustine was offered a professorship in Rome, where he founded his own school of rhetoric.

There he came under the influence of the philosophy of Plato and the teachings of St. Ambrose. After a long inner struggle, he renounced his earlier philosophical beliefs and embraced the Christian faith. He then returned to Africa where he formed a religious community. In 391 he was ordained a priest (against his wishes) as the Vandals began an

_____

_____

_____

_____

_____

_____

_____

_____

_____

_____

_____

_____

_____

_____

_____

_____

_____

_____

_____

invasion of Hippo.

For 34 years he lived in this monastic community. He wrote a vast number of books and became known for his eloquence, logic, and spiritual passion. These three combined to make Augustine one of the most significant thinkers in the history of the Christian Church. Perhaps no one except St. Paul has been so widely read for so long. His theological insights shaped not only the age he lived in, but all the subsequent centuries of Christianity. It is difficult to find a theologian—from any age—who has not been influenced by the teachings of St. Augustine.

Augustine didn't let logic hinder him in his passionate pursuit of God. It helped him. May his brief eloquence help you.

Nowhere in the Bible is the altar "the place of blessing." An altar exists for only one thing. Just ask that little lamb that was brought to the altar...this is not a place of blessing; it is a place of death. [Repentance is our altar; it is where flesh dies so the spirit can live.] But if we can embrace *that* death, then perhaps we can see God's face.

(*The God Chasers*, 55)

Day

Date

Time

Location

Fire doesn't fall on empty altars. There has to be a sacrifice on the altar for the fire to fall. If you want the fire of God, you must become the fuel of God. Jesus sacrificed Himself to win our salvation, but He has called each and every person who wants to follow Him to do what? To lay down their lives and *take up their cross* and follow Him (see Lk. 9:23).

(The God Chasers, 65)

W e need to learn how to handle the holy things of God with greater tenderness and sensitivity. We must remember that "the good" can quickly become the worst enemy of "the best." If you want God's best, then you will have to sacrifice what you think is good and acceptable. If you and I can find out what is acceptable to *Him*, "the best," then the promise of visitation becomes real.

(*The God Chasers*, 85-86)

Day

Date

Time

Location

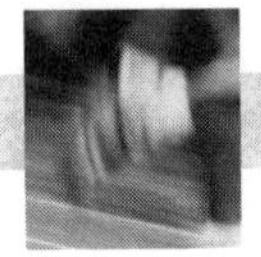

B rethren, when we finally have our meeting with God, it has to be alone in the depths of our being. We will be alone even if we are surrounded by a crowd. God has to cut every maverick out of the herd and brand him all alone. It isn't something that God can do for us en masse.

(A.W. Tozer, *The Tozer Pulpit*, Book. 8, 81, as quoted in *Worship and Entertainment*, 33)

Day

Date

Time

Location

God is calling you to a higher level of commitment. Forget the plans you've made for yourself and lay on His altar and die to self. [Flesh death is the stamp of approval on the passport to His presence.] Pray, "God, what do You want me to do?" It's time to lay everything aside and cover yourself in the blood. Nothing alive can stand in His presence. But if you're dead, then He will make you alive. So all you need to do is die if you really want to get into His presence. When the apostle Paul wrote, "I die daily," he was saying, "I enter into the presence of God every day" (see 1 Cor. 15:31b). Run in, don't run away!

_____
Day

_____
Date

_____
Time

_____
Location

(*The God Chasers*, 80-81)

_____

_____

_____

_____

_____

_____

_____

_____

_____

_____

_____

_____

_____

_____

_____

_____

_____

There is no shortcut to revival or the coming of His presence. God's glory only comes when repentance and brokenness drive you to your knees, because His presence requires purity. Only dead men see God's face. We cannot expect others to repent at that depth if you and I are not willing to continually walk in that level of repentance.

Day

Date

Time

Location

The world is tired of hearing pompous churches preaching popular sermons from behind their elevated pulpits. What right do we have to tell everybody else to repent when there are such glaring problems in our own house? Hypocrisy has never been in style in God's Church, but we've made it the main attraction in "our" version of church. What we need to do is come clean and confess, "Yes, we have some problems. Yes, *I* have some problems too. But I am repenting of my sin right now. Is there anybody here who wants to join me while I repent?"

(*The God Chasers*, 120-21)

D id you notice that *God* didn't break Mary's alabaster box? *Mary* had to break it. If you want to have that kind of encounter with God, then you will have to "break" yourself. The highest level of worship comes from brokenness, and there are no shortcuts or formulas to help you "reach the top." No one can do it for you; that is something only you can do. But if you do, God will stop just to spend time with you.

(The God Chasers, 136)

Day

Date

Time

Location

As Christ was born in a stable, and cradled in a manger, so is Christ in man ever born amidst the animals in man. The new-born Saviour is ever laid in a cradle between the ox of self-will and the ass of ignorance, in the stable of the animal condition in man; and from thence the king of pride (as Herod), finds his kingdom endangered, and seeks to kill the child, who is to become the ruler of the "New Jerusalem" in man.

(Jacob Boeme, *The Image of the Heavenly*)

_____
Day

_____
Date

_____
Time

_____
Location

_____

_____

_____

_____

_____

_____

Jacob Boeme, "chosen servant of God," was born in Alt Seidenburg, Germany, in 1575. John Wesley, in his day, required all his preachers to study the writings of Jacob Boeme; and the learned English theologian, William Law, said of him: "Jacob Boehme was not a messenger of anything new in religion, but the mystery of all that was old and true in religion and nature, was opened up to him,"—"the depth of the riches, both of the wisdom and knowledge of God."

Born of poor but pious Lutheran parents, from childhood Jacob Boeme was concerned about "the salvation of his soul." Although occupied first as a shepherd and afterward as a shoemaker, he was always an earnest student of the Holy Scriptures; but he could not understand "the ways of God." Thus he became "perplexed, even to melancholy,— pressed out of measure." He said:

"I knew the Bible from beginning to end but I could find no consolation in Holy Writ; and my spirit, as if moving in a great storm, arose in God, carrying with it my whole heart, mind and will, and wrestled with the love and mercy of God, that his blessing might descend upon me, that my mind might be illumined with his Holy Spirit, that I might understand His will and get rid of my sorrow....

"I had always thought much of how I might inherit the kingdom of heaven; but finding in myself a powerful opposition, in the desires that belong in the flesh and blood, I began a battle against my corrupted nature; and with the aid of God, made up my mind to overcome the inherited evil will,...break it, and enter wholly into

_____

_____

_____

_____

_____

_____

_____

_____

_____

_____

_____

the love of God in Christ Jesus. I sought the heart of Jesus Christ, the center of all truth; and I resolved to regard myself as dead in my inherited form, until the Spirit of God would take form in me, so that in and through Him, I might conduct my life.

"I stood in this resolution, fighting a battle with myself, until the light of the Spirit, a light entirely foreign to my unruly nature, began to break through the clouds. Then, after some farther hard fight with the powers of darkness, my spirit broke through the doors of hell, and penetrated even into the innermost essence of its newly born divinity where it was received with great love, as a bridegroom welcomes his beloved bride.

"No words can express the great joy and triumph I experienced, as of a life out of death, as of a resurrection from the dead! While in this state, as I was walking through a field of flowers, in fifteen minutes, I saw the mystery of creation, the original of this world and of all creatures....Then for seven days I was in a continual state of ecstasy, surrounded by the light of the Spirit, which immersed me in contemplation and happiness. I learned what God is and what is His will...I knew not how this happened to me, but my heart admired and praised the Lord for it!"

Jacob Boeme was a true God chaser, and he was eventually caught by what he chased. He was not content to know about God; he came to _know_ God.

63

Your brokenness is a sweet-smelling savor to God. He collects every tear that drips from your chin and flows from the corners of your eyes. The Bible says that He has a bottle of memories to hold every tear you've shed (see Ps. 56:8). He loves you, so steal away to your secret prayer place and pull out that "alabaster box" of precious anointing you've been saving for such a time as this. Break it at His feet and say, "Jesus, I love You more than anything. I'll give up anything; I'll go anywhere. I just want You, Lord."

(*The God Chasers*, 129)

_____
Day

_____
Date

_____
Time

_____
Location

The ostrich never flies,—the hen rises with difficulty, and achieves but a brief and rare flight, but the eagle, the dove, and the swallow, are continually on the wing, and soar high;—even so sinners do not rise towards God, for all their movements are earthly and earthbound. Well-meaning people, who have not as yet attained a true devotion, attempt a manner of flight by means of their good actions, but rarely, slowly and heavily; while really devout men rise up to God frequently, and with a swift and soaring wing.

(Francis de Sales, *Introduction to the Devout Life*, 3)

_____
Day

_____
Date

_____
Time

_____
Location

_____

_____

_____

_____

_____

_____

_____

_____

_____

_____

_____

_____

Francis de Sales was born into a noble family at the castle of Sales and later attended a Jesuit school in Paris. The Jesuits taught him the classics, Hebrew, Greek, and the life of discipline. His training also included the study of law and the humanities. He was ordained as a priest in 1591, despite opposition from his family. In 1602 he became the bishop of Geneva.

Francis was a prolific writer whose works had a great influence on the Church. He combined spiritual growth with ethical concern in a way that few writers, before or after him,

_____

_____

_____

_____

_____

_____

_____

_____

_____

_____

_____

_____

_____

_____

_____

_____

_____

_____

_____

_____

have been able to do. He was a master of metaphor, describing the mysteries of the spiritual life through simple, everyday images like bees and milk, birds and sugar. Because of his considerable influence, Francis is considered to be one of the "doctors of the Western Church."

I often use simple stories of my children as de Sales did of life around him to communicate deep truth. To pursue God is pretty simple. Let's not make it complicated. It's simple, but passionate!

Happy the man who gives himself to God! Happy are they who throw themselves with bowed head and closed eyes into the arms of the "Father of mercies," and the "God of all consolation"....

There is only one way to love God, that is not to take one step without him, and to follow with a brave heart wherever he leads.

(Fénelon, *Christian Perfection*, 65, 67-68)

Day

Date

Time

Location

True religion is evermore a powerful thing; and the power of it appears, in the first place in the inward exercises of it in the heart where is the principal and original seat of it. Hence true religion is called the *power of godliness.*

The business of religion is from time to time compared to those exercises, wherein men are wont to have their hearts and strength greatly exercised and engaged....

...everyone that has the power of godliness in his heart, has his inclinations and heart exercised towards God and divine things, with such strength and vigor that these holy exercises do prevail in him above all carnal or natural affections, and are effectual to overcome them....

(Jonathan Edwards, Religious Affections)

Day
Date
Time
Location

Jonathan Edwards was a Congregational pastor and a key figure in the eighteenth-century "Great Awakening." He is considered to be one of America's greatest theologians. Born in Connecticut and educated at Yale, he ministered for 23 years at a church in Northampton, Massachusetts. He later became a missionary to the Indians at Stockbridge. In 1758 he was named president of Princeton University, but died only a few weeks after taking office.

Edwards produced a theology of Christian spirituality for his age that blended together Lockean philosophy and his own Calvinist theology. His main concern was the question, "How do we distinguish the presence of the Holy Spirit?" Christian experience, according to Edwards, is a gift of God, but he spent his life working out the ways in which we define that experience. A central theme of his writings—evidenced in the following selection—is the importance of religious "affections," which he defined as the passions that move the will to act.

My study of Jonathan Edwards' life probably affected me more than his writings. Early in my ministry I contemporized and preached his famous sermon "Sinners in the hands of an angry God," but my preaching what he wrote did not have the same effect on myself or on my listeners. Meeting *who* he wrote and preached about had incredible effect. May we have another "Great Awakening" by meeting Edwards' "Great Awakener."

M any souls become addicted to the spiritual sweetness of the devotional life and strive to obtain more and more of it.

People who fancy themselves as spiritual are quite often not pleased to hear about the spiritual growth of others.

Such souls become weary with spiritual exercises because they do not yield any consolation....

No soul will ever grow deep in the spiritual life unless God works passively in that soul by means of the dark night.

(St. John of the Cross, excerpts from *The Dark Night of the Soul*)

Day

Date

Time

Location

The spiritual giants of old were men who at some time became acutely conscious of the real Presence of God and maintained that consciousness for the rest of their lives. The first encounter may have been one of terror, as when a "horror of great darkness" fell upon Abram, or as when Moses at the bush hid his face because he was afraid to look upon God. Usually this fear soon lost its content of terror and changed after a while to delightsome awe, to level off finally into a reverent sense of complete nearness to God. The essential point is, *they experienced God.*

(A.W. Tozer, *The Divine Conquest*, 26-27, as quoted in *Worship and Entertainment*, 55)

Day

Date

Time

Location

Whatever else it embraces, true Christian experience must always include a genuine encounter with God. Without this, religion is but a shadow, a reflection of reality, a cheap copy of an original once enjoyed by someone else of whom we have heard. It cannot but be a major tragedy in the life of any man to live in a church from childhood to old age with nothing more real than some synthetic god compounded of theology and logic, but having no eyes to see, no ears to hear and no heart to love.

(A.W. Tozer, *The Divine Conquest*, 26, as quoted in *Worship and Entertainment*, 56)

Day

Date

Time

Location

So then in the beginning man loves God, not for God's sake, but for his own....But when tribulations, recurring again and again, constrain him to turn to God for unfailing help, would not even a heart as hard as iron, as cold as marble, be softened by the goodness of such a Savior, so that he would love God not altogether selfishly, but because He is God?...Thereupon His goodness once realized draws us to love Him unselfishly, yet more than our own needs impel us to love Him selfishly.

(Bernard of Clairvaux, *On Loving God*, Chapter IX)

———————————————
Day

———————————————
Date

———————————————
Time

———————————————
Location

Bernard was one of the great leaders in the history of the Church. He was an eloquent speaker and was considered by many to be one of the holiest individuals who ever lived. He grew up in Dijon, France, and at the age of 22 entered as a novice in the monastery of Citeaux. Three years later he was appointed to supervise a group of his fellow monks in the newly founded monastery at Clairvaux. Though he was offered high positions in the Church, Bernard remained at Clairvaux until his death.

Thanks to careful preservation over the centuries, many of Bernard's writings have survived today. His works had a profound influence on both Martin Luther and John Calvin. It is obvious that Bernard cared more about Heaven's opinion than Earth's. Lord, make us like that!

A nd then our Lord opened my spiritual eye and shewed me my soul in midst of my heart. I saw the Soul so large as it were an endless world, and as it were a blissful kingdom. And by the conditions that I saw therein I understood that it is a worshipful City. In the midst of that City sitteth our Lord Jesus, God and Man, a fair Person of large stature, highest Bishop, most majestic King, most worshipful Lord; and I saw Him clad majestically. And worshipfully He sitteth in the Soul, even-right in peace and rest. And the Godhead ruleth and sustaineth heaven and earth and all that is,—sovereign Might, sovereign Wisdom, and sovereign Goodness,—[but] the place that Jesus taketh in *our Soul* He shall never remove it, without end, as to my sight....

(Julian of Norwich, *Revelations of Divine Love*, 168)

Day

Date

Time

Location

ulian is the most popular of the English mystics. She lived as a Benedictine nun in Norwich, beside the St. Julian Church, from which she most likely took her name. Little is known about Julian's life, although she is mentioned by her contemporary, Margery Kempe.

Julian's book, *Revelations of Divine Love*, entitled her to become the first great female writer in the English language. Despite her disclaimers of being unskilled as an author, she wrote lively prose in a style all her own. She was well trained in the Bible as well as in the teachings of the Church.

Her theology is based on her mystical experiences. She became seriously ill at the age of 30 and, in the midst of her suffering, prayed for a vision of Christ's passion. Once in a time of prayer Julian heard the words, "I am the foundation of your praying"—words that

_____

_____

_____

_____

_____

_____

_____

_____

_____

_____

_____

_____

_____

_____

_____

_____

_____

_____

greatly influenced her spiritual life. She always pointed to the goodness and love of God, a light in a time of darkness for Julian, who lived in an age of social unrest and the fear of the Black Plague.

Joy is perhaps the keynote in her writings. She penned the famous saying, "All shall be well and all shall be well, and all manner of things shall be well." Her writings have been called "the most perfect fruit of later medieval mysticism in England."

If having a "mystical" experience disqualifies you, then Paul/Saul would be disqualified. Encounters with God within the framework and boundaries of His written Word have always been what the true seeker searches for. Paul compared his "mystically" derived theology with Peter's, and it "differed not a whit." Pursue God and confirm what you find in His Word.

I *love them that love Me; and those that seek Me early shall find Me* (Proverbs 8:17).

His forgiveness is for all; His love flows to those who love Him. One cannot love Him without being loved by Him. This is the promise to God chasers: Seek Him diligently and you will "catch" Him. Run, son, run!

(Tommy Tenney)

_____
Day

_____
Date

_____
Time

_____
Location

W̲e want God to change the world. But He cannot change the world until He can change us. In our present state we are in no position to *affect* anything. But if we will submit to the Master Potter, He will make us—all of us—into what He needs us to be. He may remake the vessel of our flesh many times, but if we will submit to the Potter's touch, He can turn us into vessels of honor, power, and life. After all, wasn't He the One who turned unlearned fishermen into world-changers and hated tax collectors into fearless revivalists? *If He did it once, He can do it again!*

(The God Chasers, 101)

	Day
	Date
	Time
	Location

Accordingto the first Law of Motion: Every body continues in its state of rest, or of uniform motion in a straight line, except in so far as it may be compelled *by impressed forces* to change that state. This is also a first law of Christianity. Every man's character remains as it is, or continues in the direction in which it is going, until it is compelled *by impressed forces* to change that state. Our failure has been the failure to put ourselves in the way of the impressed forces. There is a clay, and there is a Potter; we have tried to get the clay to mould the clay.

(Henry Drummond,
The Greatest Thing in the World and Other Addresses)

Day

Date

Time

Location

Henry Drummond (1851–1897), a professor at Edinburgh University in Scotland, had an inherent love for and broadly developed interests in natural science and religion. He strove to convey to others those glimpses of a wider outlook and flashes from a penetrating insight that had cheered and illuminated his own solitary path.

Of all the books that have been written about love, perhaps none have been as influential and inspirational as *The Greatest Thing in the World*. Based on the thirteenth chapter

_____

_____

_____

_____

_____

_____

_____

_____

_____

_____

_____

_____

_____

_____

_____

_____

_____

_____

_____

_____

of First Corinthians, this classic message has directed millions of people to the way of true happiness. The simple beauty and positive truths of this dynamic sermon will encourage readers to practice the power and blessing of God's supreme gift to mankind: love.

I first received a copy of this little book when I was 16 years old. Its words impacted me so much that today I can still quote from Henry Drummond.

He will not frustrate us. God will allow Himself to be caught by us. As a father playing tag with his child allows himself to be caught by the laughing, loving child, so too will the heavenly Father allow Himself to be caught. In fact, just when you would tire in despair, He will turn and catch you. He wants to be "captured" by our love. He eagerly awaits the laughing, loving encounter. He has missed those times with man since the Garden. Intuitively, God chasers have known this. *They were willing to chase the "uncatchable," knowing the "impossible" would catch them.* In fact, one famous God chaser wrote this:

I follow after, if that I may apprehend *that for which also I am apprehended of Christ Jesus* (Philippians 3:12b).

(The God Chasers, 151)

Day

Date

Time

Location

*N*evertheless when it shall turn to the Lord, the veil shall be taken away (2 Corinthians 3:16).

Day

Date

Time

Location

One can turn away from sin without turning toward the Lord. The result is just a "good" person. One who not only turns away from sin but who also turns in absolute dependence to the Lord becomes a "god" person. The veil is removed when you turn toward the person of Jesus. When you walk in the blindness of the letter of the law, an encounter with the Person of the law will open the eyes of your heart. Ask Paul of Tarsus about Saul of Tarsus.

(Tommy Tenney)

"You can't get there from here." So I've been told. Then I must build a road—a highway, a road of repentance! Then I can "get there"! Where is *there*? In His presence.... Isaiah said it and John the Baptist repeated it: "The voice of him that crieth in the wilderness, Prepare ye the way of the Lord, make straight in the desert a highway for our God" (Is. 40:3). Build the road of repentance and you get the "King's Highway"—a passageway of His presence to your person.

(Tommy Tenney)

_____ Day

_____ Date

_____ Time

_____ Location

G od doesn't want us to turn away from His glory so we can build pitiful monuments to a momentary revelation we never paid for with our tears. *Salvation is a free gift, but God's glory will cost us everything.* He wants us to press in and *live* in His perpetual habitation of glory. He wants us to be so saturated with His presence and glory that we carry His presence with us everywhere we go in this life. This may be the only way the unspeakable glory of God will find its way to the shopping malls, hair style salons, and grocery stores of our nation.

(*The God Chasers,* 150-51)

Day

Date

Time

Location

W e can't expect the lost and the hurting to come running to our "river" only to discover that there's barely enough for them to get a single sip from God's glass. We've told them, "God is really here; there's food on the table," but every time they have believed our report, they have been forced to comb through the carpet for the mere crumbs of the promised feast. *Our past is more powerful than our present.*

(*The God Chasers*, 30)

G od is tired of screaming instructions at the Church; He wants to guide us with His eye [see Ps. 32:8]. That means we have to be close enough to Him to see His face. He's tired of correcting us through public censure. We have sought His hands for too long. We want what He can do for us; we want His blessings, we want the chills and the thrills, we want the fishes and the loaves. Yet we shirk at the high commitment it takes to pursue His face.

(The God Chasers, 47)

Day

Date

Time

Location

The Cinderella of the church of today is the prayer meeting. This handmaid of the Lord is unloved and unwooed because she is not dripping with the pearls of intellectualism, nor glamorous with the silks of philosophy; neither is she enchanting with the tiara of psychology. She wears the homespuns of sincerity and humility and so is not afraid to kneel!

(Leonard Ravenhill, *Why Revival Tarries*)

_____
Day

_____
Date

_____
Time

_____
Location

_____

_____

_____

_____

_____

_____

_____

_____

_____

_____

_____

_____

_____

_____

_____

Leonard Ravenhill was a powerful preacher and author of many stirring books, including the classic, *Why Revival Tarries*. He was one of England's outstanding evangelists.

He also was a man most intimate with his God. His manner of writing is biting at times, and frequently harsh. But it never was an arbitrary harshness. The harshness was from the raw conviction that the words convey. His writings were clearly from the throne.

Brother Len went to be with the Lord on Thanksgiving Day weekend, 1994.

_____

_____

_____

_____

_____

_____

_____

_____

_____

_____

_____

_____

_____

_____

_____

_____

_____

_____

_____

_____

_____

_____

_____

The quote in this journal is one that has been locked into my memory banks since I was 16 years old. He ignited the flame of passion in my heart with words like, "We need more agonizers than we need organizers."

Leonard impacted me, with his words, more than anyone I know. May his words strike a flame in your heart!

Y ou need to forget who's around you and abandon the "normal protocol." God is in the business of re-defining what we call "church" anyway. He's looking for people who are hot after His heart. He wants a Church of Davids who are *after* His own heart (not just His hand). (See Acts 13:22.) You can seek for His blessing and play with His toys, or you can say, "No, Daddy, I don't just want the blessings; I want You. I want You to come close. I want You to touch my eyes, touch my heart, touch my ears, and change me, Lord. I'm tired of me the way I am, because if I can change, *then the cities can change too."*

(The God Chasers, 64)

Day

Date

Time

Location

You may be in the same place I am in today. I've been in too many ark-less church services. I've endured too many powerless choir songs. I'm even tired of my own ministry! I have preached too many sermons that may have been anointed but didn't usher in the very presence of the One we all long for. Maybe I was doing the best I knew how to do, but all I could do was muster up a faint scent of Him, the merest hint of something immeasurably better and more powerful.

(*The God Chasers*, 87-88)

Day

Date

Time

Location

God struck down Uzzah right on the spot and stopped David's parade in its tracks. *God broke out of His box and caused man's plans to fall* that day, and it would take David three months to recover, repent, research, and return for God's glory. The same thing happens today when we encounter God's manifest glory. Too often we reach out in fleshly presumption to stop the God we've carefully contained in a box from falling off of our rickety man-made ministry program or tradition. We shouldn't be surprised when God's glory breaks out of our doctrinal or traditional boxes and shocks us. Something always dies when God's glory encounters living flesh.

(The God Chasers, 92-93)

The Lord knows that we have tried to pave the way for people to come to God through painless, cheap grace and costless revival. But all we wound up with was bargain basement salvations that hardly lasted a week. Why? Because all we gave people was an emotional encounter with man when what they really needed was a death encounter with the glory and presence of God Himself.

(*The God Chasers*, 117)

Day

Date

Time

Location

I think we will all be surprised at the number of people who will start crawling out from the crevices of society when they see the Church repenting! Once again, it all goes back to our most serious problem—we don't have the bread of His presence. Our churches are filled with "career prodigals" who love their Father's things more than their Father. We come to the family dinner table not to ask for more of the Father, but to beg and persuade Him to give us all the things in His house that He promised are rightfully ours. We open the Book and lick our lips and say, "I want all the gifts, I want the best portion, the full blessing; I want all that belongs to me." Ironically, it was the father's blessing that actually "financed" the prodigal son's trip away from the Father's face! And it was the son's new revelation of his poverty of heart that propelled him back into his Father's arms.

(The God Chasers, 121)

Day

Date

Time

Location

M any modern saints spend a lot of time looking for shortcuts to God's glory. *We want the gain without the pain.* We want revival in our cities, but we don't want to hear anyone tell us that revival only comes when people are hungry, when "vicarious intercessors" repent for sins they never committed on behalf of people they've never met. Paul said, "For I could wish that myself were accursed from Christ for my brethren, my kinsmen according to the flesh" (Rom. 9:3).

(The God Chasers, 148)

Day

Date

Time

Location

Y**ou must learn to love the cross. He who does not love the cross does not love the things of God. (Matthew 16:23) It is impossible for you to truly love the Lord without loving the cross. The believer who loves the cross finds that even the bitterest things that come his way are sweet. The Scripture says, "To the hungry soul every bitter thing is sweet." (Proverbs 27:7)

Here is a true spiritual principle that the Lord will not deny: God gives us the cross, and then the cross gives us God.

(Madame Jeanne Guyon, *Experiencing the Depths of Jesus Christ*, 38)

_____
Day

_____
Date

_____
Time

_____
Location

M**adame Jeanne Guyon** was born at Montargis, France. When she was only 15, she married an invalid who was 38 years old. Unhappy in her marriage, she sought happiness in her devotional life. She lived in a convent under royal order for a year and then was imprisoned in Vincennes and the Bastille because of her religious beliefs. Almost 25 years of her life were spent in confinement. Many of her books were written during that period.

Writing that compels the reader to move into a living experience of Jesus Christ is

Madame Guyon's great contribution to devotional literature. *Experiencing the Depths of Jesus Christ* (sometimes titled *A Short and Very Easy Method of Prayer*) has had a wide influence: Watchman Nee saw that it was translated into Chinese and made available to every new convert in the Little Flock; François Fénelon, John Wesley, and Hudson Taylor all highly recommended it to the believers of their day.

This book has had powerful personal impact on me.

W ill we dare to draw close to His glory? God really wanted the children of Israel to come up and receive the Ten Commandments directly from Him along with Moses. But they ran from God's presence. The Church is in danger of doing the same thing today. We can take the risk of something dying in us as we dare to draw close to His glory, or we can turn and run back to our traditions of men and the safety of religious legalism and man-operated church services. *Seeker-friendly is fine; Spirit-friendly is fire!*

(*The God Chasers*, 150)

_____
Day

_____
Date

_____
Time

_____
Location

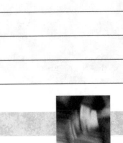

W hen the anointing of God rests on human flesh, it makes everything flow better. One of the clearest pictures of the anointing and its purpose in the Bible is provided in the Book of Esther. When Esther was being prepared for her presentation to the king of Persia, she was required to go through a year of purification during which she was repeatedly soaked in fragrant anointing oil (ironically using virtually the same ingredients of the Hebrews' worship incense and anointing oil). *One year in preparation for one night with the king!* A logical side benefit of all those soaking baths in perfumed oil is that *every man* who came near to Esther would think or say, "My, but you smell good." Nevertheless, Esther wouldn't give them the time of day for the same reason that you and I should never be distracted by the pursuit of man's approval:

Day

Date

Time

Location

The purpose of the anointing is not to make man like you, but to make the King like you.

(The God Chasers, 41)

118

I have a strong sense that God is about to strip all that away to ask us, "Now, who loves *Me*? Who wants *Me*?" It's time to seek the Reviver instead of revival!

God is tired of having *long distance relationships* with His people. He was tired of it thousands of years ago in Moses' day, and He is tired of it today. He really wants to have intimate, close encounters with you and me. He wants to invade our homes with His abiding presence in a way that will make every visitor begin to weep with wonder and worship the moment they enter.

(The God Chasers, 75)

Day

Date

Time

Location

At once I knew that my dear Saviour stood before me. I rose at once from the rock where I was seated and fell at His feet. He held in His hand the key of my heart. Opening the inner chamber of my heart with His key of love, He filled it with His presence, and wherever I looked, inside or out, I saw but Him.

Then did I know that man's heart is the very throne and citadel of God, and that when He enters there to abide, heaven begins.

(Sadhu Sundar Singh, *At the Master's Feet*)

Day _____

Date _____

Time _____

Location _____

_____
_____
_____
_____
_____
_____
_____
_____
_____
_____

Sadhu Sundar Singh has been called the St. Paul of India. His conversion to Christ is one of the great stories of the faith. Sundar was raised a Sikh, so he had studied intently the holy book of the Sikh religion, the Granth Sahib, as well as the Hindu sacred book, the Gita. His piety even as a child was known throughout the region.

Sundar's mother died when he was just a teenager, and her death threw the young man into overwhelming grief. He railed at God, even publicly burning the Bibles of the Christian missionaries of the area.

Finally, Sundar's despair led him to plan his own death. For three days and nights he stayed in his room. "If God wants me to live, let Him say so," he exclaimed. "Oh God, if there be a God, reveal Yourself to me tonight." His plan was simple and carefully thought out: If God did not speak to him before morning, he would go out to the railway line, lay his head on the rails, and wait in the darkness for the 5:00 a.m. train from Ludhiana to end his misery. For seven hours he waited in silent meditation. At 4:45 a.m., witnesses Sundar, a bright cloud of light suddenly filled his room, and out of the brightness came the face and figure of Jesus. Sundar had been expecting Krishna or one of his own gods, not Jesus. Yet, he was certain it was Jesus. He spoke to Sundar in Hindustani: "How long are you going to persecute Me? I died for you. For you I gave My life. You were praying to know the right way; why don't you take it? I am the Way."

As a result of this vision, Sundar's life was dramatically and irrevocably changed, and he was led into one of the most remarkable ministries of the twentieth century.

Hot hunger can lead to holy encounters. Fan the flames of your hunger!

Take with you words, and turn to the Lord: say unto Him, Take away all iniquity, and receive us graciously: so will we render the calves of our lips (Hosea 14:2).

Day

Date

Time

Location

Hear the plea of God! He is not impressed with your gold. He wants your words. They beguile His heart. Human words can cause Heaven's throne to stop the sun. Ask Hezekiah. God collects our prayers and tears. They're the only things on earth that are presently in Heaven. When we entice Him with our words, it allows entrance into the "throne zone." Pray!

(Tommy Tenney)

You may be only a few spiritual inches away from the encounter of a lifetime. If you want to see the face of God, then just follow Mary to the feet of Jesus. Pull out your alabaster box of precious sacrificial praise and worship. You've been holding your treasure back for too long, but there is One here who is worthy of it all. Don't hold anything back!

(*The God Chasers*, 128)

Day

Date

Time

Location

Jesus said that this woman who had broken her alabaster box to anoint Him for His burial would never be forgotten wherever the gospel is preached. In other words, *she would always be on God's mind.* Do you want a visitation from God? You will have to make room for Him in your life, no matter how crowded and cluttered it may be at this moment. Sometimes it means your most treasured things may have to be broken to release the fragrance God remembers.

(*The God Chasers,* 129)

Day

Date

Time

Location

I wonder if, when Mary broke open the alabaster box...she noticed that when her tears fell on our Lord's dusty, unwashed feet, that they made a streak of cleanliness? Did it suddenly dawn upon her what measure of disrespect had been shown toward Jesus...? I believe she did, and it broke her heart. Her grief seemed to only turn up the velocity of her tears until they came like a floodgate had been opened....Mary was literally able to use them to wash away the animal dung on His feet!

But what could Mary use to wipe the remaining residue...? ...Having nothing else at hand, with no towels provided by servant or master, Mary dismantled her hair and used her glory [see 1 Cor. 11:15] to wipe Jesus' feet....She removed every evidence of His public rejection with her beautiful hair and took it as her own. *Can you imagine what that did for the heart of God?* [While she washed His feet, He cleansed her reputation.]

(*The God Chasers*, 131)

Day

Date

Time

Location

130

G od spoke to me and said, "Mary dismantled her glory to minister to Me." If all the
disciples were present, there were at least 12
other people in that room that day, and not
one of them attained the intimacy that she
obtained that day. The disciples missed it,
even though they were good people like
Peter, James, and John. Hear me, friend; you
can be busy being a disciple and *doing the
work*, but *miss the worship*! Do you really think God needs us to *do things*
for Him? Isn't He the Creator who stepped out on the balcony of Heaven
and scooped out the seven seas with the palms of His hands? Wasn't it God
who pinched the earth to make the mountains? Then obviously He doesn't
need you to "do" anything. What He wants is your *worship*. Jesus told the
woman at the well, "...true worshippers shall worship the Father in spirit,
and in truth: for *the Father seeketh such to worship Him*" (Jn. 4:23). [This is
what the Father is actively seeking: humble worshipers.]

(*The God Chasers*, 132)

Day
Date
Time
Location

We "pedestalize" people whom God has anointed. Whom does God memorialize? Jesus says that what Mary did will "be told for a memorial of her" (Mt. 26:13). We like the anointed; He likes the "anointers"! These are people of His face and feet—oil pourers, tear washers, humble lovers of Him more than lovers of His things. [They will gladly take the marriage vow—"for richer or poorer," abased or abounding. They are in love with Him!]

(*The God Chasers*, 133)

Day

Date

Time

Location

E very great spiritual work from Paul to this hour has sprung out of spiritual experiences that made worshipers. Unless we are worshipers, we are simply religious dancing mice, moving around in a circle getting nowhere....

God wants worshipers first. Jesus did not redeem us to make us workers; He redeemed us to make us worshipers. And then, out of the blazing worship of our hearts springs our work.

(A.W. Tozer, from a sermon quoted in
Worship and Entertainment, 19)

Day

Date

Time

Location

G od will whisper His prophetic secrets be- fore they ever come to pass for broken- box worshipers and fragrant anointers. He will turn aside at the height of His glory for people who will dismantle their own glory and ego just to share His shame as their own.

(*The God Chasers*, 135)

Day

Date

Time

Location

God is calling. The first time God revealed this to me, I trembled and wept in front of the people as I told them the same thing I tell you today: "You are at Mount Sinai today, and God is calling you into personal intimacy with Him. If you dare to answer His call, then it is going to redefine everything you've ever done." Your decision today will determine whether you go forward or backward in your walk with Christ.

Day

Date

Time

Location

Intimacy with God requires a certain level of brokenness because purity comes from brokenness. The games are over, friend. He's calling you.

(The God Chasers, 80)

Bibliography

Augustine, St. *Confessions.* Albert C. Outler, trans. and ed., 1955. May 5, 1999. <http://ccel.wheaton.edu/a/augustine/confessions/confession-bod.html>.

Bernard of Clairvaux. *On Loving God.* May 5, 1999. <http://ccel.wheaton.edu/b/bernard/loving_God/loving_God-bod.html>.

Boeme, Jacob. *The Image of the Heavenly.* August 28, 1998. April 30, 1999. <www.sigler.org/boeme/index.htm>.

de Sales, Francis. *Introduction to the Devout Life.* London, Oxford, Cambridge: Rivingtons, 1876. May 13, 1999. <http://ccel.wheaton/edu/d/desales/dvout_life/devout_life/html>.

Drummond, Henry. *The Greatest Thing in the World and Other Addresses.* 1998. May 4, 1999. <http://ccel.wheaton.edu/d/drummond/greatest/thing18.htm>.

Edwards, Jonathan. *Religious Affections.* May 4, 1999. <http://ccel.wheaton.edu/e/edwards/religious_affections/affections1.0.html>.

Fénelon, François de Salignac de la Mothe. *Christian Perfection.* Minneapolis, MI: Bethany House Publishers, 1975; publ. in arrangement with Harper & Row, Inc., New York, 1947.

—. *Spiritual Progress.* New York: M.W. Dodd, 1853. April 30, 1999. <http://ccel. wheaton.edu/f/fenelon/progress/spirit02.htm>.

Guyon, Jeanne. *Experiencing the Depths of Jesus Christ.* Gene Edwards, ed. Gardiner, ME: Christian Books Publishing House, 1975.

John of the Cross, St. *The Dark Night of the Soul.* Excerpts taken from *Devotional Classics,* eds. Richard J. Foster and James Bryan Smith. HarperSanFrancisco. Copyright 1990, 1991, 1993 by RENOVARÉ. 33-36.

Julian of Norwich. *Revelations of Divine Love.* Grace Warrack, ed. London: Methuen & Co. Ltd, 1901. May 5, 1999.<http://ccel.wheaton.edu/j/julian/ revelations/revelations.html>.

Lewis, C.S. *Mere Christianity.* Excerpts taken from *Devotional Classics,* eds. Richard J. Foster and James Bryan Smith. HarperSanFrancisco. Copyright 1990, 1991, 1993 by RENOVARÉ. 7-10.

Ravenhill, Leonard. *Why Revival Tarries.* Minneapolis, MN: Bethany House Publishers, 1979. May 5, 1999. <http://www.accsoft.com.au/~clcoz/whyrevta.htm>.

Tenney, Tommy. *The God Chasers.* Shippensburg, PA: Destiny Image Publishers, 1998.

Tozer, A.W. *The Divine Conquest,* as quoted in Tozer, *Worship and Entertainment.* Camp Hill, PA: Christian Publications, 1997.

—. *The Tozer Pulpit,* as quoted in Tozer, *Worship and Entertainment.* Camp Hill, PA: Christian Publications, 1997.

—. *Tozer on Worship and Entertainment: Selected Excerpts.* comp. James L. Snyder. Camp Hill, PA: Christian Publications, 1997.

Singh, Sadhu Sundar. *At the Master's Feet.* Rev. Arthur and Mrs. Parker, trans. London and Edinburg: Fleming H. Revell Co., 1922. April 30, 1999. <http://ccel.wheaton.edu/s/singh/feet/feet05.htm>.

Join the Chase

There are millions of GodChasers around the world today helping ignite fire in the hearts of people who are hungry for the presence of God. Join the Chase by getting connected with *GodChasers.network.*

Once you contact us, we will send you our monthly newsletter FREE! This will help you stay informed about upcoming GodChaser Gatherings around the world, new resources by Tommy & Jeannie Tenney to share with you and the impact GodChasers around the world are making in our world today.

Sign up by calling or writing to:

**Tommy Tenney
GodChasers.network
Post Office Box 3355
Pineville, Louisiana 71361-3355
USA**

318-44CHASE (318.442.4273)

or sign up online at www.GodChasers.net

Visit us on the web @ www.godchasers.net for more information such as:

- Upcoming events in your area.
- Monthly E-letters with special offers on GodChasers products.
- "Daily dose" of scripture portions that will enable you to read through the Bible in a year by email.
- Become a prayer partner.
- New books and other product releases by Tommy Tenney.
- Online daily devotions by Tommy Tenney.
- And much more!

Run With Us!

Become a GodChasers.network Monthly Seed Partner

"Have you caught Him yet?"

We're asked a lot of questions like that— and with a name like "God-Chasers.network," we've come to expect it! Do we really think that we can "catch" God? Is God running away from us? What are we talking about?

"God chasers" are people whose hunger for Him compels them to run—not walk—towards a deeper and more meaningful relationship with the Almighty. For them, it isn't just a casual pursuit. Sundays and Wednesday nights aren't enough: they need Him every day, in every situation and circumstance, the good times and the bad.

Chasing God in our troubled times isn't always easy, but if we're really seeking God, and not just His blessings, then our cicumstances shouldn't hinder our pursuit. We will find God in trying times and learn that He is in control even when everything around us seems to be spinning out of control. He may *seem* distant from us...but when we pursue Him, we'll find that He *wants* us to "catch" Him, and He will draw near. That's what "chasing God" is all about!

Are you a "God chaser"? If the cries of your heart are echoed in the words of this message, would you prayerfully consider "running with us" as a GodChasers.network partner? Each month, our Seed Partners who sow into this ministry with a monthly gift of $20 or more receive a teaching tape. It's a small token of our gratitude, and helps our partners stay current with the direction and flow of the ministry.

Thank you for your interest in **GodChasers.network**. We look forward to chasing Him with you!

In Pursuit,

Tommy Tenney

Tommy Tenney
& The GodChasers.network Staff

Become a Monthly Seed Partner
by calling or writing to:

Tommy Tenney
GodChasers.network
P.O. Box 3355
Pineville, Louisiana 71361-3355
318.44CHASE (318.442.4273)

◆ T R A I N I N G
◆ E Q U I P P I N G
◆ M E N T O R I N G
◆ L A U N C H I N G

Join the GodChasers Intern Program today...
...and start changing your future!

THE GODCHASERS.NETWORK INTERNS is a 9-month program that will intensify your hunger in pursuit of God's presence and desire to foster unity in the body of Christ. Also available: A short-term (8-weeks) summer boot camp.

It will give you the opportunity to experience and train in the day-to-day operations of a world-impacting ministry. This experience will help cultivate godly character and integrity while working in the vineyard of the Lord!

I would love to hear from you. Please visit **www.godchasers.net** and share your thoughts and ideas with me.

Tony Tenney

*If You Enjoyed This Book
By Tommy Tenney,
Don't Miss His Fiction Debut...*

HADASSAH
One Night With the King

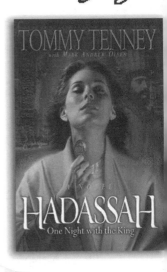

The incredibly gripping story of Esther is now expanded into a powerful, full-length novel full of passion, pathos, and adventure!

Against a vividly painted historical, geo-political backdrop, bestselling author Tommy Tenney breathes new life into the heart-stopping tale of Hadassah, a simple peasant girl who is chosen over 127 more qualified candidates to become Esther, queen of Persia. Was it her beauty alone, or had she discovered an important and mysterious truth?

Based on extensive historical research, Tenney takes readers to pre-Islamic Persia to uncover the secrets that helped Esther win the heart and gain the ear of the king—and ultimately to save her people.

Both a palace thriller and Jewish memoir, the novel's layers of suspense and intrigue capture the imaginations of both male and female readers as Tenney leads them from war zones into the place, behind closed doors where only the most favored may enter....

Ideal for giving to family and friends, Christian and Jews, who may not ever have read a "religious" book before. Order your copies of this high-stakes page turner now!

Made into a Major Motion Picture!

1-888-433-3355 or visit *www.godchasers.net*

BOOKS BY

Tommy Tenney

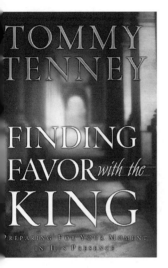

Finding Favor with the King

Book-New Release now available in paperback!

Esther's ultimate secret...Have you ever needed a "that night" or maybe a that day"? A point in time where things are going wrong, but after which, they go right? Understanding what goes into creating "that moment" of divine favor was Esther's ultimate secret.

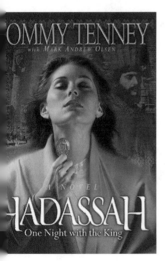

Hadassah: One Night with the King

Book- New Release now available in paperback!

A gripping action-adventure story full of political intrigue and suspense, with a brand new perspective on a historical figure that you already know. Hadassah brings the age-old story of Esther to Life!

BOOKS BY

[signature: Tommy Tenney]

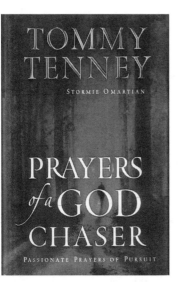

Prayers Of A God Chaser
Book- Video teaching series available through GodChasers.network

In Prayers Of A God Chaser, Tommy Tenney shares prayers- and principles of prayer- from the Bible that have revolutionized his life & relationship with God. His passionate, heartf response to the prayers of Jesus, David, Hann & others will inspire & transform your praye life. Let Tommy Tenney lead you into God's presence & you will learn to pray anew.

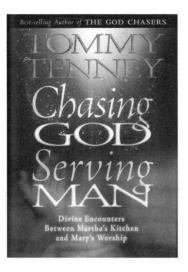

Chasing God Serving Man
Book- Audio teaching series available through GodChasers.network

Using the backdrop of Bethany & the hou of Mary & Martha, Tommy Tenney biblic explores new territory. The revolutionary concepts in this book can change your lif You will disover who you really are (and unlock the secret of who "they" really are

Other resources by Tommy Tenney, such as audio tapes, CD's, videos, & other books can be purchased by calling:
1-888-433-3355 or by visiting us online at:
www.godchasers.net

Also available...music by Jeannie Tenney!

More titles
by Tommy Tenney

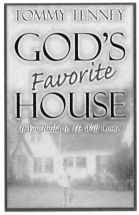

Other books endorsed
by Tommy Tenney

━ **DIGGING THE WELLS OF REVIVAL** by Lou Engle

Foreword—Within our history lies our hope. *Digging the Wells of Revival* draws our attention to the spiritual inheritance of our country. From Azusa Street in Los Angeles at the turn of the century, to Toronto, Baltimore, and Brownsville as we face the next century, Lou Engle reminds us that what was, can be what is—where waters once flowed freely, they can again spring forth in this generation.
ISBN 0-7684-2015-6

━ **A DIVINE CONFRONTATION** by Graham Cooke

Foreword—If you choose to read this book, you should probably throw out your old ecclesiastical dictionary. Nothing is as it seems…it's bigger and better. Only we didn't know it! And Graham Cooke told us. Change is coming! The spiritual climate is about to be radically altered. Thank you, Graham, for "forthtelling" the spiritual weather patterns.
ISBN 0-7684-2039-3

━ **THEY DRANK FROM THE RIVER AND DIED IN THE WILDERNESS** by David Ravenhill

Foreword—Move from the place of *privilege* to the place of *purpose*, from the people of God *among* the nations, to the priests of God *to* the nations. The river is not the goal! It's a "gate"! Cross and enter—God's promises are in the promised land! Wildness is in the wilderness! The wilderness is only the *bridge* between slavery and sonship—Egypt and Canaan. Don't die en route!
ISBN 0-7684-2038-5

━ **NO MORE SOUR GRAPES** by Don Nori

Don Nori has masterfully passed on to us the lessons of true fatherhood. He states powerfully: "The children's deliverance is locked up in the parents' repentance." Amen, Father Don! I agree! I repent! *No more sour grapes!*
ISBN 0-7684-2037-7

━ **THE LOST PASSIONS OF JESUS** by Donald L. Milam, Jr.

This book is on fire! To be left unchanged you'd have to read it with asbestos gloves and an iceberg heart.
ISBN 0-9677402-0-7

Available at your local Christian bookstore.

For more information and sample chapters, visit www.reapernet.com

Other books endorsed
by Tommy Tenney

― **FATHER, FORGIVE US!** by Jim W. Goll
This book is a road map to restoring the power and passion of forgiveness.
How could we have neglected it so long? *Father, forgive us!*
ISBN 0-7684-2025-3

― **THE RELEASE OF THE HUMAN SPIRIT** by Frank Houston
The bindings on this book cover must be extra strong! That's the only thing
I know that keeps this book from 'exploding'! Are you ready to release
your spirit? To go to the next level?
ISBN 0-7684-2019-9

― **THE MARTYRS' TORCH** by Bruce Porter
The Body of Christ will be eternally grateful for what the pastor and par-
ents of Rachel Scott share in this book. "There shall be light at evening
time" (see Zech. 14:7b). We can see the future by the bright light of *The
Martyrs' Torch.*
ISBN 0-7684-2046-6

― **THE RADICAL CHURCH** by Bryn Jones
He calls for a heavenly harmony where earth begins to sing on pitch with
heaven's tune...where man prays the Lord's prayers instead of man's
prayers. In Bryn's words, "Is it not time for passionate prophetic confrontation again?"
ISBN 0-7684-2022-9

― **POWER, HOLINESS, AND EVANGELISM** by Randy Clark
The future of the Church is at stake and this book has some answers. These
authors speak eloquently, confirming what you have felt, affirming what
you intuitively knew.
ISBN 1-56043-345-0

Available at your local Christian bookstore.

**For more information and sample chapters,
visit www.reapernet.com**

Books to help you grow strong in Jesus

▬ TODAY GOD IS FIRST
by Os Hillman.
Sometimes it is hard to keep Him first in my day. It is a struggle to see Him in the circumstances of my job. I need help to bring the reality of my Lord into my place of work. Os Hillman has the uncanny ability to write just to my circumstance, exactly to my need. He helps me see God's view. He strengthens my faith and courage to both see God and invite Him into the everyday trials and struggles of work. Take this book to work, put it on your desk or table. Every day just before you tackle the mountains before you, pause long enough to remind yourself—Today, God is First.
ISBN 0-7684-2049-0

▬ THE ASCENDED LIFE
by Bernita J. Conway.
A believer does not need to wait until Heaven to experience an intimate relationship with the Lord. When you are born again, your life becomes His, and He pours His life into yours. Here Bernita Conway explains from personal study and experience the truth of "abiding in the Vine," the Lord Jesus Christ. When you grasp this understanding and begin to walk in it, it will change your whole life and relationship with your heavenly Father!
ISBN 1-56043-337-X

▬ EXTRAORDINARY POWER FOR ORDINARY CHRISTIANS
by Erik Tammaru.
Ordinary people don't think too much about extraordinary power. We think that this kind of power is for extraordinary people. We forget that it is this supernatural power that makes us all extraordinary! We are all special in His sight and we all have the hope of extraordinary living. His power can change ordinary lives into lives empowered by the Holy Spirit and directed by His personal love for us.
ISBN 1-56043-309-4

▬ THE THRESHOLD OF GLORY
compiled by Dotty Schmitt.
What does it mean to experience the "glory of God"? How does it come? These women of God have crossed that threshold, and it changed not only their ministries but also their very lives! Here Dotty Schmitt and Sue Ahn, Bonnie Chavda, Pat Chen, Dr. Flo Ellers, Brenda Kilpatrick, and Varle Rollins teach about God's glorious presence and share how it transformed their lives.
ISBN 0-7684-2044-X

Available at your local Christian bookstore.

For more information and sample chapters, visit www.reapernet.com

Books to help you grow strong in Jesus

◄━━━ THE HIDDEN POWER OF PRAYER AND FASTING
by Mahesh Chavda.
The praying believer is the confident believer. But the fasting believer is the overcoming believer. This is the believer who changes the circumstances and the world around him. He is the one who experiences the supernatural power of the risen Lord in his everyday life. An international evangelist and the senior pastor of All Nations Church in Charlotte, North Carolina, Mahesh Chavda has seen firsthand the power of God released through a lifestyle of prayer and fasting. Here he shares from decades of personal experience and scriptural study principles and practical tips about fasting and praying. This book will inspire you to tap into God's power and change your life, your city, and your nation!
ISBN 0-7684-2017-2

◄━━━ THE LOST ART OF INTERCESSION
by Jim W. Goll.
Finally there is something that really explains what is happening to so many folk in the Body of Christ. What does it mean to carry the burden of the Lord? Where is it in Scripture and in history? Why do I feel as though God is groaning within me? No, you are not crazy; God is restoring genuine intercessory prayer in the hearts of those who are open to respond to His burden and His passion.
ISBN 1-56043-697-2

◄━━━ ENCOUNTERING THE PRESENCE
by Colin Urquhart.
What is it about Jesus that, when we encounter Him, we are changed? When we encounter the Presence, we encounter the Truth, because Jesus is the Truth. Here Colin Urquhart, best-selling author and pastor in Sussex, England, explains how the Truth changes facts. Do you desire to become more like Jesus? The Truth will set you free!
ISBN 0-7684-2018-0

◄━━━ WORSHIP: THE PATTERN OF THINGS IN HEAVEN
by Joseph L. Garlington.
Worship and praise play a crucial role in the local church. Whether you are a pastor, worship leader, musician, or lay person, you'll find rich and anointed teaching from the Scriptures about worship! Joseph L. Garlington, Sr., a pastor, worship leader, and recording artist in his own right, shows how *worship is the pattern of things in Heaven*!
ISBN 1-56043-195-4

◄━━━ RELEASERS OF LIFE
by Mary Audrey Raycroft.
Inside you is a river that is waiting to be tapped—the river of the Holy Spirit and power! Let Mary Audrey Raycroft, a gifted exhorter and teacher and the Pastor of Equipping Ministries and Women in Ministry at the Toronto Airport Christian Fellowship, teach you how you can release the unique gifts and anointings that the Lord has placed within you. Discover how you can move and minister in God's freeing power and be a releaser of life!
ISBN 1-56043-198-9

Available at your local Christian bookstore.

For more information and sample chapters, visit www.reapernet.com

6B-1:12

Books to help you grow strong in Jesus

LADY IN WAITING
by Debby Jones and Jackie Kendall.
This is not just another book for single women! The authors, both well-known conference speakers, present an in-depth study on the biblical Ruth that reveals the characteristics every woman of God should develop. Learn how you can become a lady of faith, purity, contentment, patience—and much more—as you pursue a personal and intimate relationship with your Lord Jesus!
ISBN 1-56043-848-7
Devotional Journal and Study Guide
ISBN 1-56043-298-5

FROM THE FATHER'S HEART
by Charles Slagle.
This is a beautiful look at the true heart of your heavenly Father. Through these sensitive selections that include short love notes, letters, and prophetic words from God to His children, you will develop the kind of closeness and intimacy with the loving Father that you have always longed for. From words of encouragement and inspiration to words of gentle correction, each letter addresses times that we all experience. For those who diligently seek God, you will recognize Him in these pages.
ISBN 0-914903-82-9

AN INVITATION TO FRIENDSHIP: From the Father's Heart, Volume 2
by Charles Slagle.
Our God is a Father whose heart longs for His children to sit and talk with Him in fellowship and oneness. This second volume of intimate letters from the Father to you, His child, reveals His passion, dreams, and love for you. As you read them, you will find yourself drawn ever closer within the circle of His embrace. The touch of His presence will change your life forever!
ISBN 0-7684-2013-X

DON'T DIE IN THE WINTER...
by Dr. Millicent Thompson.
Why do we go through hard times? Why must we suffer pain? In *Don't Die in the Winter...* Dr. Thompson, a pastor, teacher, and conference speaker, explains the spiritual seasons and cycles that people experience. A spiritual winter is simply a season that tests our growth. We need to endure our winters, for in the plan of God, spring always follows winter!
ISBN 1-56043-558-5

UNDERSTANDING THE DREAMS YOU DREAM
by Ira Milligan.
Have you ever had a dream in which you think God was speaking to you? Here is a practical guide, from the Christian perspective, for understanding the symbolic language of dreams. Deliberately written without technical jargon, this book can be easily understood and used by everyone. Includes a complete dictionary of symbols.
ISBN 1-56043-284-5

Available at your local Christian bookstore.

For more information and sample chapters, visit www.reapernet.com

6B-1:13